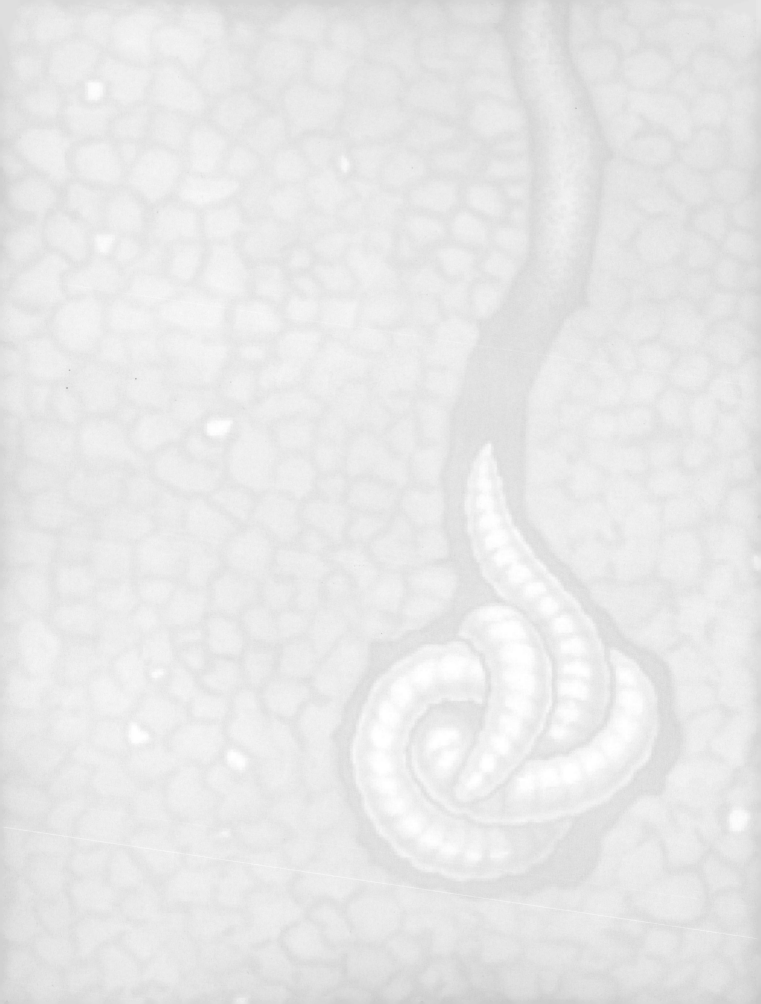

Earthworms

CLAIRE LLEWELLYN • BARRIE WATTS

W
FRANKLIN WATTS
A Division of Scholastic Inc.
NEW YORK TORONTO LONDON AUCKLAND SYDNEY
MEXICO CITY NEW DELHI HONG KONG
DANBURY, CONNECTICUT

First published in 2000 by Franklin Watts
96 Leonard Street, London EC2A 4XD

First American edition 2002 by Franklin Watts
A Division of Scholastic Inc.
90 Sherman Turnpike
Danbury, CT 06816

Text and artwork © 2000 Franklin Watts
Photography © 2000 Barrie Watts

Series Editor: Anderley Moore
Editor: Rosalind Beckman
Series Designer: Jason Anscomb
Illustrator: David Burroughs

Catalog details are available from the Library of Congress
Cataloging-in-Publication Data

ISBN 0-531-14651-0 (lib. bdg.) 0-531-14825-4 (pbk.)

Printed in China

Contents

All Sorts of Worms   6–7

Finding Earthworms   8–9

A Worm's Body   10–11

Feeding   12–13

Moving   14–15

Tunneling   16–17

Mating   18–19

Hatching   20–21

Enemies   22–23

Food for Birds   24–25

Worm Wonders!   26–27

Glossary   28

Index   29

All Sorts of Worms

Dig up any patch of earth in a garden or park. Look closely and you will probably see a wriggly worm.

Worms that live in the soil are called earthworms. There are several kinds of earthworms.

Most earthworms are reddish-brown and about as long as your hand.

There are many different kinds of worms around the world. Worms come in many colors and sizes. Some are so tiny that they are hard to see. Others, such as the giant earthworm of Australia, are as long as a car!

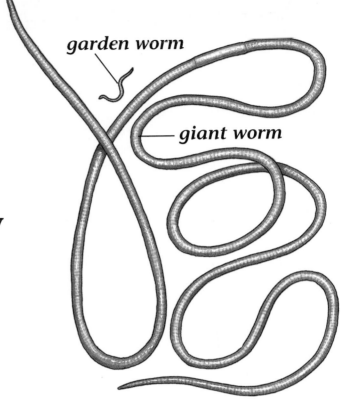

garden worm

giant worm

This giant worm from Australia is as long as a car! It is much larger than a garden worm.

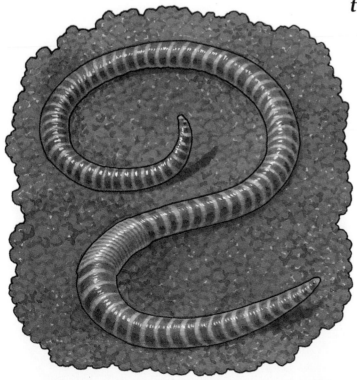

◀ The brandling worm has a stripy skin. This makes it easy to recognize.

Finding Earthworms

Earthworms live in damp soil where there are bits of dead plants to eat. Most of them live near the top of the soil.

Earthworms are easy to find. Dig in the garden with a spade or fork. You are sure to find some in the soil.

Earthworms live in woods, meadows, and gardens. They live under lawns and among dead leaves under bushes and trees. Worms also love compost heaps, where people pile vegetable peelings and other food waste.

There are very few worms in sandy soil. This is because rainwater drains away quickly, and the soil becomes too dry for them.

A Worm's Body

A worm is a very simple animal. It has no skeleton, no lungs, no eyes, and no ears. Its body is a tube made of many tiny segments. Each segment is filled with liquid and has bristles that help the worm move.

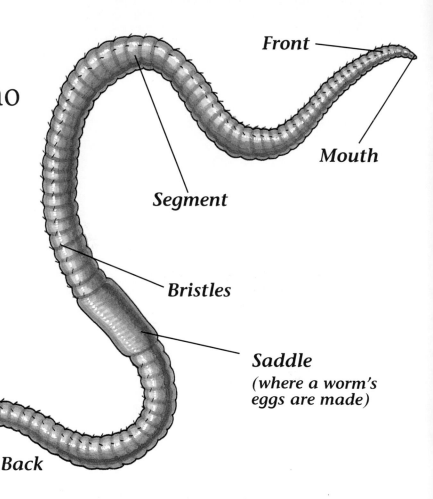

Front

Mouth

Segment

Bristles

Saddle
(where a worm's eggs are made)

Back

Worms can tell the difference between light and dark. If a worm is uncovered, it tries to get back in the dark.

Earthworms breathe through their skins. They take in air that is trapped in the soil.

On wet days, worms' air pockets fill with water, and worms have to go up to the surface. If they didn't, they would drown underground.

A worm's body is damp but not slimy. The front end is more pointed than the back.

Feeding

Earthworms feed on the rotting parts of dead plants. They have no teeth or jaws, so the food they eat has to be very soft. Sometimes they nibble food with their tiny lips, but usually they suck it up.

◄ Worms also feed on soil. They use the good parts as the soil goes through their body. Then they get rid of waste in a worm cast.

In the daytime, worms usually stay under the soil and feed on the roots of dead plants. At night, when it is dark and damp, they crawl up to the surface and search for dead leaves. They drag the leaves under the ground.

A pile of dead leaves is a favorite feeding place for worms. Sometimes they store the leaves in their tunnels until they rot. This makes the soil healthy.

Moving

Worms have strong muscles to help them move. There are ring-shaped muscles inside each segment. These make their body shrink or spread out. Other muscles run along their body, and make it grow short or long.

A worm's damp body helps it move easily through the soil.

A worm's bristles are very important in helping it move. The worm digs its bristles into the soil to anchor itself.

1 *A worm moves by pointing its head in the direction it wants to go. It anchors the back of its body, and the head end becomes thicker.*

2 *The worm then stretches its body to push through the soil. It anchors the front of its body and brings up the rear.*

Tunneling

A worm makes tunnels by pushing its way into the soil and eating it. As the worm moves forward, its body coats the soil with slime. This makes the tunnels stronger, but they soon collapse.

A worm tunneling its way through the soil

Worm tunnels make airy spaces under the soil. These spaces help rainwater drain away. The soil becomes looser and finer, so it is easier for plants to grow.

Some worms burrow deeper underground when the weather is too cold or too dry. They push down to a few feet below the surface, then coil up and go to sleep. They wake up when the weather gets better.

This worm is sleeping through a hot, dry summer in a burrow deep underground.

Mating

Worms like to mate on warm, damp nights. The two worms lie next to each other and wrap themselves together with slime. They stay close like this for several hours.

After mating, the saddle on each worm makes a sticky belt of slime. The worm wriggles out of its belt and lays its eggs in it. The belt turns into a hard cocoon. It is smaller than a pea.

A close-up of the saddle, where a worm's eggs are made. Worms have to mate with each other to make eggs. Every worm has both male and female parts to its body, so any worm it meets can be a mate.

Hatching

Worms' eggs take many weeks or months to grow in the cocoon. In that time, some of the eggs will die. Sometimes just one or two worms hatch out of the cocoon.

A worm's cocoon

Young earthworms are about as long as a thumbnail. They are whiter than their parents, and they have no saddles at first. Otherwise they look just the same.

▲
Adult worm with young worms

It takes eighteen months for a young worm to grow up and lay eggs of its own. If it doesn't get eaten, the worm may live in the soil for ten years or more.

Enemies

Worms have many enemies, such as hedgehogs and shrews. Both of these animals are active at night when worms come out to feed.

A mole is an earthworm's greatest enemy. Moles sometimes eat thirty worms a day as they tunnel under the ground. They store extra worms in a special pantry.

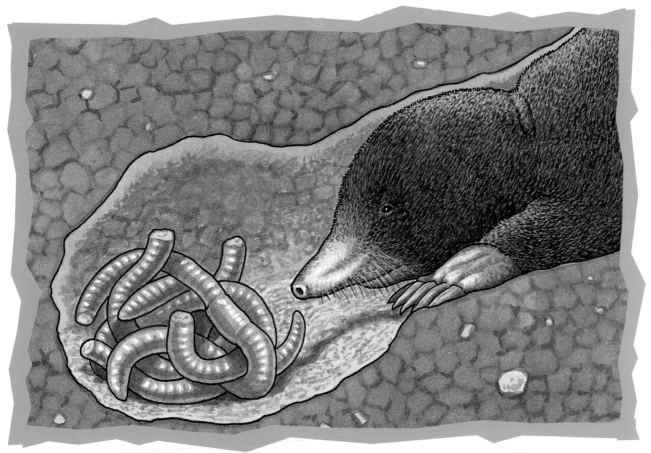

A mole's pantry full of worms

Moles keep worms from escaping from their pantry by biting off their heads. This does not kill the worm. Its head grows again, and the worm might be able to escape!

Food for Birds

Many birds eat worms. Robins, blackbirds, and thrushes all visit gardens and parks. They look and listen for the tiny movements of earthworms in the ground.

When a bird finds a worm, it grabs it by the tail. Worms are hard to pull out of the soil. The worm anchors itself in the ground with its bristles and pulls back hard with its powerful muscles.

A fight between a bird and a worm is just like tug-of-war.

Birds hunt for worms in the spring when other food is scarce. As plants ripen in the summer and fall, birds usually leave worms alone.

Worm Wonders!

There are over 1,800 different kinds of worms around the world.

A medium-sized garden has about twenty thousand earthworms.

A worm's body is made up of about 250 segments.

A famous scientist named Charles Darwin believed that the worm is the world's most important animal because it helps plants grow.

Without worms, the soil would be wet, heavy, and hard to dig.

Worms eat about one-third of their body weight every day. That's like a person eating twenty loaves of bread!

Every crumb of soil in parks and gardens has passed through the body of a worm.

Worm casts are very good for the garden. The soil in them is very fine and has valuable food from plants.

Earthworm farms sell worms to gardeners to help them improve their soil.

Fish like to eat juicy worms. That's why fishers use worms as bait.

Worms have blood but no heart.

Glossary

bristle a tiny, stiff hair

cocoon the hard, oval case where a worm's eggs grow

compost heap a place where people pile dead plants and fruit and vegetable peelings. These plants rot to become compost, which is used to feed the soil.

muscle the part of an animal's body that helps it move

saddle the swollen part of an adult worm's body where the eggs are made, and which it uses during mating to make a cocoon

shrew a small animal that looks like a mouse but has a longer nose

worm cast the soil that passes out of a worm's body and makes a little pile on the grass

Index

birds 24, 25
body 10, 11
brandling 7
breathing 11
bristles 10, 15, 25, 28

cocoon 19, 20, 28
compost 9, 28

Darwin, Charles 26

eggs 19, 20, 21
 belt 19
enemies 22, 23, 24, 25

feeding 12, 13, 27
fish 27

giant earthworm 7

hedgehog 22

mating 18, 19
mouth 10
moles 23
muscle 14, 25, 28

saddle 10, 19, 21, 28
segments 10, 14, 26
shrew 22, 28
skin 7, 11
sleeping 17
slime 16, 18, 19
soil 6, 8, 9, 11, 12, 13,
 15, 16, 17, 21, 26, 27

tunneling 16, 17

worm cast 12, 28

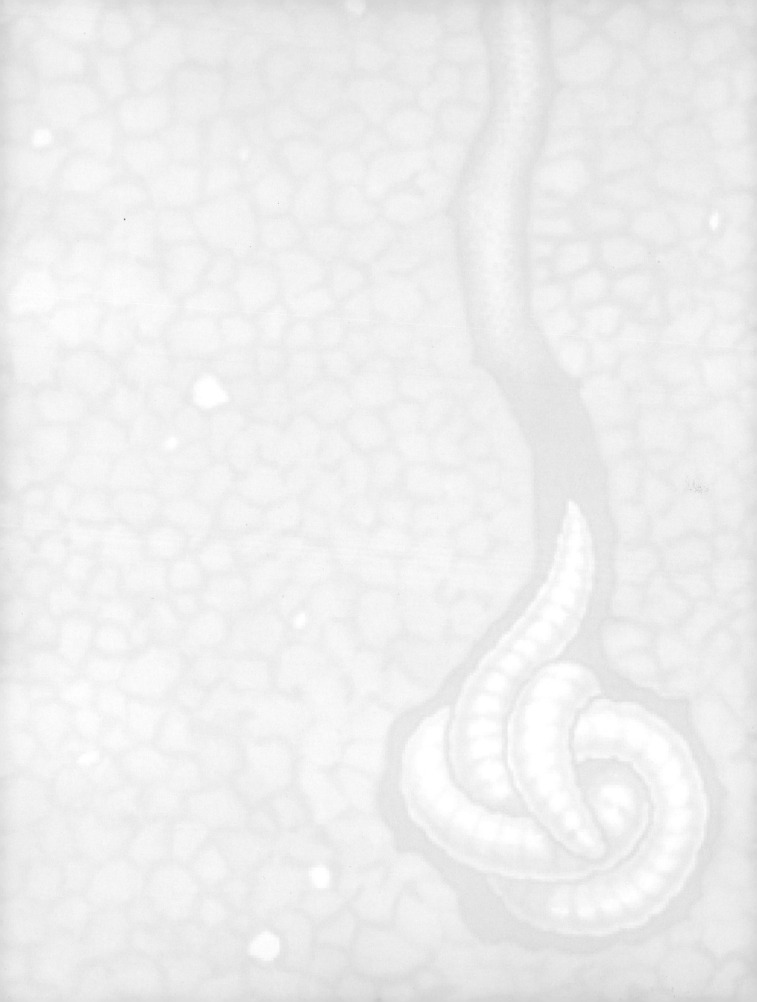